Conrad K. Butler

Speed Legends:
The Quickest Cars from Every Brand

Conrad K.
PUBLISHING WAW

Cars are incredible marvels of technology that captivate the imagination and curiosity of people of all ages. From the sleek designs of sports cars to the raw power of hypercars, there's something undeniably thrilling about the pursuit of speed.

Have you ever wondered which BMW model is the fastest? Or which Mazda holds the title of being the fastest to ever leave their factory? In this book, you set out on a journey to discover what is the fastest road-legal car from the most popular manufacturers. These cars represent the pinnacle of automotive engineering, pushing the boundaries of what's possible on the road and leaving us in awe of their performance capabilities. Whether breaking speed records on the track or turning heads on the road, these cars serve as a testament to human innovation and ingenuity.

The maximum speeds listed here are current for 2024, but it's important to remember that technology is always evolving, and new cars may soon break these records. Some older models still hold the title for top speed, showing the lasting impact of their design and engineering.

Various factors influence the maximum speed of a vehicle, each playing a crucial role in determining its top velocity. Engine power stands as a fundamental determinant, with higher horsepower engines capable of propelling the vehicle to greater speeds. Aerodynamics also significantly impact maximum speed, as sleek designs reduce air resistance, allowing the vehicle to cut through the air more efficiently.

Additionally, factors such as weight distribution and tire grip play vital roles, with lighter weights and optimal tire traction contributing to improved acceleration and higher top speeds. Overall, it's the synergy of these factors that ultimately determines the maximum speed a vehicle can achieve. While I can't cover every car brand in existence, I have carefully selected the most iconic and noteworthy ones to feature in this book. Each brand represents a unique chapter in automotive history, showcasing the passion, innovation, and dedication of engineers and designers across the globe. So, buckle up and prepare for an exhilarating ride!

The GMC Hummer EV is a powerful, all-electric supertruck. It features an impressive 1,000 horsepower and accelerates from 0 to 60 mph in just about 3 seconds. Despite its might, it has a top speed of only... 105 mph. This is not surprising, because this colossus weighs as much as 9046 lbs!

TATA Harrier

The TATA Harrier is the fastest car in the TATA lineup, with a top speed of 121 mph. Its stylish design and spacious interior provide comfort for drivers and passengers alike. The Harrier exemplifies TATA's commitment to blending performance, innovation, and style in one remarkable vehicle.

The SUZUKI Kizashi is the fastest car in the SUZUKI lineup, reaching a top speed of 133 mph. This sedan combines solid performance with a sleek, stylish design. It offers a comfortable and spacious interior, making it suitable for both everyday driving and longer trips. The Kizashi highlights SUZUKI's ability to blend speed and comfort in a single vehicle.

FIAT 124 Spider

The FIAT 124 Spider, with a top speed of 144 mph, is the fastest car in the FIAT lineup. Weighing just over 2,400 pounds, this lightweight roadster is powered by a 1.4-liter turbocharged engine. It delivers 160 horsepower, providing an exhilarating driving experience. The 124 Spider combines classic design with modern performance, showcasing FIAT's engineering excellence.

The CITROEN C5 V6 Biturbo reaches a top speed of 149 mph, making it the fastest car in the CITROEN lineup. Powered by a 3.0-liter V6 engine, it produces an impressive 240 horsepower. This model combines high performance with a comfortable and spacious interior, suitable for both city driving and long trips.

PEUGEOT RCZ R

The PEUGEOT RCZ R is the fastest car in the PEUGEOT lineup, with an electronically limited top speed of 155 mph. With a 1.6-liter turbocharged engine producing 270 horsepower, it offers impressive performance. This model can accelerate from 0 to 60 mph in just 5.9 seconds, highlighting its sporty capabilities. The same electronic speed limitation applies to the next few cars in this book with a top speed of 155 mph, ensuring a balance between power and safety.

The SEAT Cupra, SEAT's fastest model, features a manufacturer-limited top speed of 155 mph. Equipped with a powerful engine, it offers thrilling performance on the road. Its dynamic design and responsive handling make every drive an exciting experience.

SKODA Octavia vRS

The SKODA Octavia vRS, the pinnacle of speed in the SKODA lineup, boasts an electronically limited top speed of 155 mph. Powered by a robust engine, it accelerates from 0 to 60 mph in just 6.6 seconds, offering impressive performance. With its sleek design and sporty features, the Octavia vRS provides a dynamic driving experience and safety.

VOLVO
top varieties

Many VOLVO models are capable of reaching speeds above 155 mph, but they are electronically limited to this speed for safety reasons. For example, the Volvo S60 T8 Polestar Engineered (pictured above), with its powerful hybrid engine, has the potential to exceed this limit. Despite this, Volvo prioritizes safety, ensuring that all their high-performance models remain within a controlled top speed.

SUBARU WRX STI

The legendary SUBARU WRX STI S209 holds the title as the fastest car in the SUBARU lineup, with a maximum speed of 161 mph. Weighing approximately 3,485 pounds, it features a 2.5-liter turbocharged engine that produces 341 horsepower. This powerful engine allows the S209 to accelerate from 0 to 60 mph in just around 4.9 seconds. Combining high performance with precise handling, the WRX STI S209 is a standout model for driving enthusiasts.

The BUICK Regal GS, the fastest car in the BUICK lineup, reaches a top speed of 162 mph. It is powered by a 3.6-liter V6 engine that delivers 310 horsepower. This performance-oriented sedan can accelerate from 0 to 60 mph in just about 5.4 seconds. With its combination of speed, power, and elegance, the Regal GS stands out in BUICK's range of vehicles.

RENAULT Megane RS Trophy-R

The RENAULT Megane RS Trophy-R is the fastest car in RENAULT's lineup, with a top speed of 162 mph. Featuring a 1.8-liter turbocharged engine, it produces an impressive 300 horsepower. This lightweight model, weighing around 2,920 pounds, excels in agility and handling. Its performance capabilities make the Megane RS Trophy-R a standout choice for driving enthusiasts.

The KIA Stinger GT, with a top speed of 167 mph, is the fastest car in KIA's lineup. It is equipped with a 3.3-liter twin-turbo V6 engine that generates 365 horsepower. This powerful sedan can accelerate from 0 to 60 mph in just 4.7 seconds, showcasing its impressive performance. It is the only car with sports aspirations in the Korean manufacturer's lineup.

VOLKSWAGEN Golf R "20 years"

Celebrating two decades of performance, the VOLKSWAGEN Golf R "20 years" edition is the fastest car in the brand's history, reaching a top speed of 167 mph. It features a 2.0-liter turbocharged engine that produces an impressive 328 horsepower. This special edition model stands out with exclusive design elements and enhanced performance features.

The MAZDA RX-8 Spirit R, with a top speed of 169 mph, is the fastest car in MAZDA's lineup. It features a unique Wankel rotary engine that produces 232 horsepower. This special edition model is known for its lightweight design and exceptional handling. Combining speed with innovative engineering, the RX-8 Spirit R stands out as a remarkable achievement in MAZDA's history.

CHRYSLER 300C SRT-8 6.4 HEMI

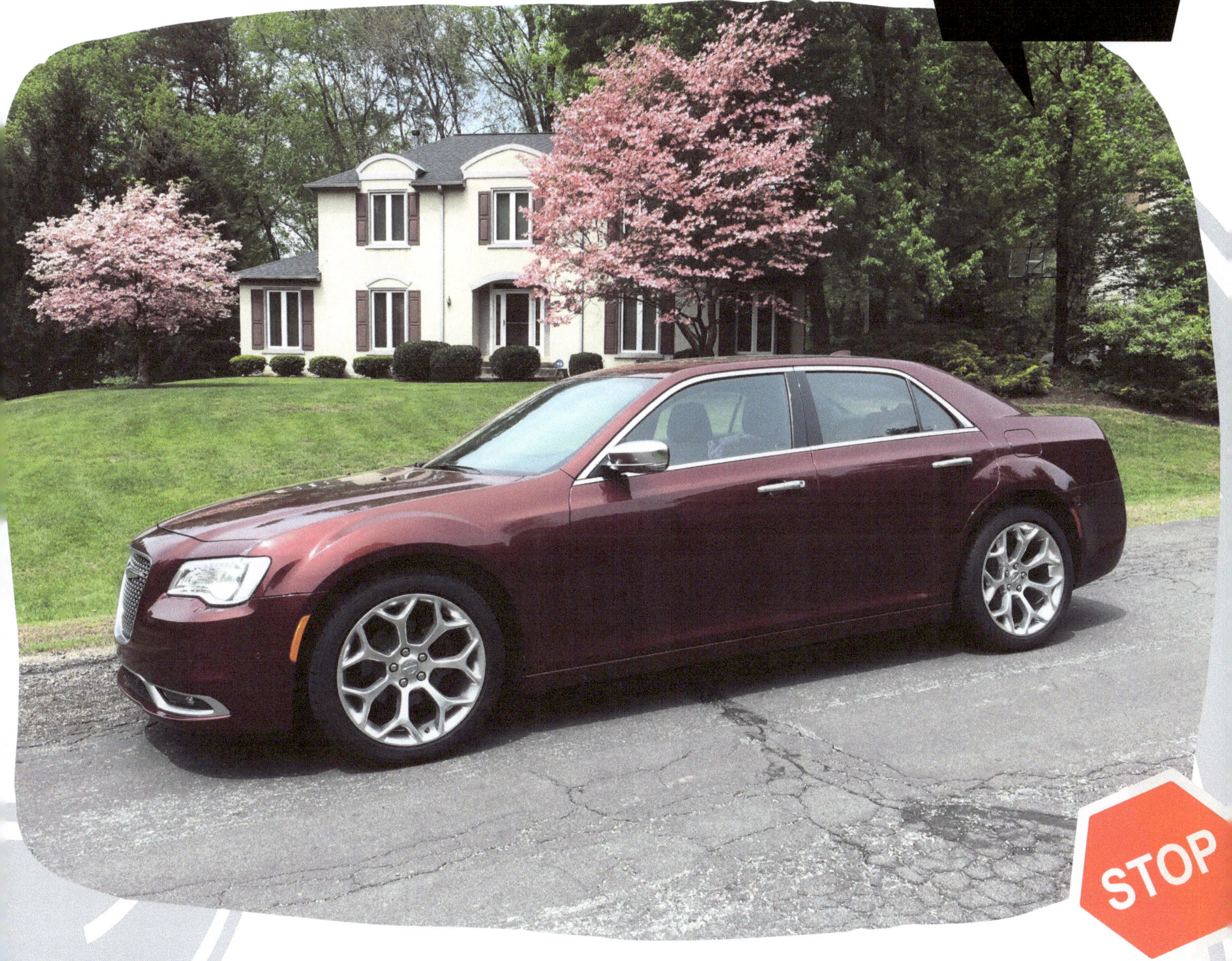

The CHRYSLER 300C SRT-8 6.4 HEMI is the fastest car in the CHRYSLER lineup, with a top speed of 174 mph. It's powered by a 6.4-liter HEMI V8 engine that produces 470 horsepower. Known for its muscular performance, this model can accelerate from 0 to 60 mph in just 4.3 seconds. Its blend of speed, power, and classic design makes the 300C SRT-8 a standout in the CHRYSLER range.

MITSUBISHI Lancer Evo

With a top speed of 175 mph, the MITSUBISHI Lancer Evo FQ400 is the fastest car in the MITSUBISHI lineup. It boasts a 2.0-liter turbocharged engine that generates an impressive 411 horsepower. Acceleration is another strong point, as it can go from 0 to 60 mph in just 3.8 seconds. This model is celebrated for its exceptional handling and performance, making it a standout among high-performance sedans.

OPEL Lotus Omega

The OPEL Lotus Omega reaches a top speed of 175 mph, making it the fastest car in the OPEL lineup. For a time, it held the title of the fastest sedan in the world. Its 3.6-liter twin-turbocharged engine produces 377 horsepower, delivering remarkable performance. The car was originally produced in only one color, "Imperial Green", a very dark green.

The JEEP Grand Cherokee Trackhawk, with a top speed of 179 mph, is the fastest vehicle in the JEEP lineup. Powered by a 6.2-liter supercharged V8 engine, it generates an impressive 707 horsepower. This high-performance SUV can accelerate from 0 to 60 mph in just 3.5 seconds.

RANGE ROVER
Sport SV

The RANGE ROVER Sport SV holds the title of the fastest car in the Land Rover lineup, with a top speed of 180 mph. It is equipped with a 5.0-liter supercharged V8 engine that produces 575 horsepower. This high-performance SUV can accelerate from 0 to 60 mph in just 4.3 seconds. Combining luxury and speed, the Sport SV offers an unparalleled driving experience both on and off-road.

HONDA NSX
type S

The HONDA NSX Type S is the fastest car in the HONDA lineup, reaching a top speed of 190 mph. This supercar is powered by a 3.5-liter twin-turbo V6 engine paired with three electric motors, delivering a combined output of 600 horsepower. It can accelerate from 0 to 60 mph in just 2.9 seconds, showcasing its remarkable performance capabilities. Additionally, the car features advanced aerodynamics and lightweight materials, enhancing both speed and handling.

BMW M4 CSL

The BMW M4 CSL reaches a top speed of 190 mph, making it the fastest car in the BMW lineup. Equipped with a 3.0-liter twin-turbo inline-six engine, it produces 543 horsepower. This high-performance model can accelerate from 0 to 60 mph in just 3.6 seconds. Notably, the M4 CSL incorporates extensive use of lightweight materials, significantly enhancing its agility and driving dynamics.

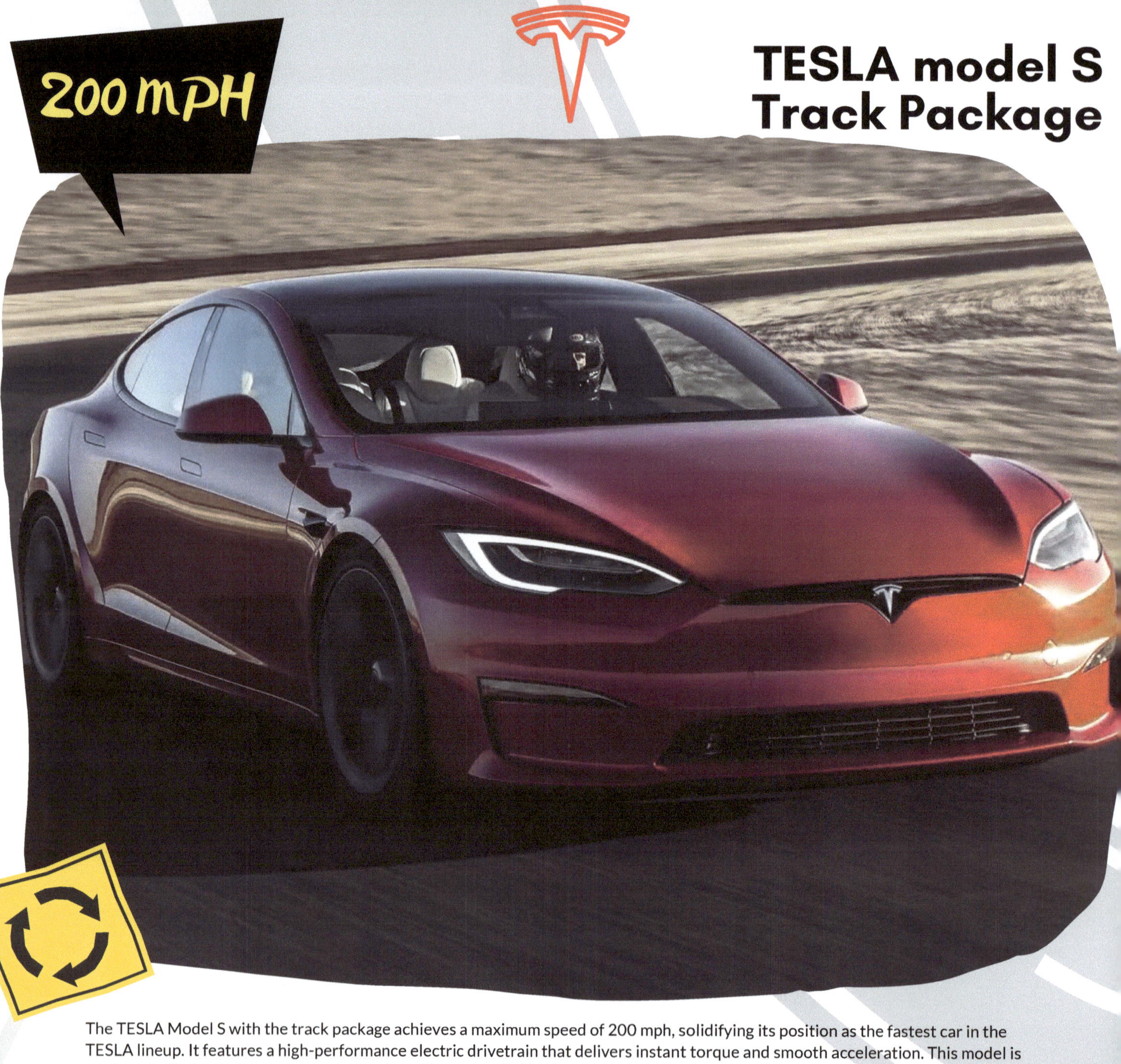

The TESLA Model S with the track package achieves a maximum speed of 200 mph, solidifying its position as the fastest car in the TESLA lineup. It features a high-performance electric drivetrain that delivers instant torque and smooth acceleration. This model is equipped with track-focused enhancements such as upgraded brakes and suspension for improved handling and stability at high speeds.

CADILLAC CT5-V Blackwing

The CADILLAC CT5-V Blackwing boasts a top speed of 200 mph, securing its place as the fastest car in the CADILLAC lineup. Powered by a high-performance V8 engine, it delivers exhilarating power and acceleration. With its advanced chassis and suspension tuning, the CT5-V Blackwing offers exceptional handling and agility. This luxury sedan combines speed, comfort, and cutting-edge technology for an unparalleled driving experience.

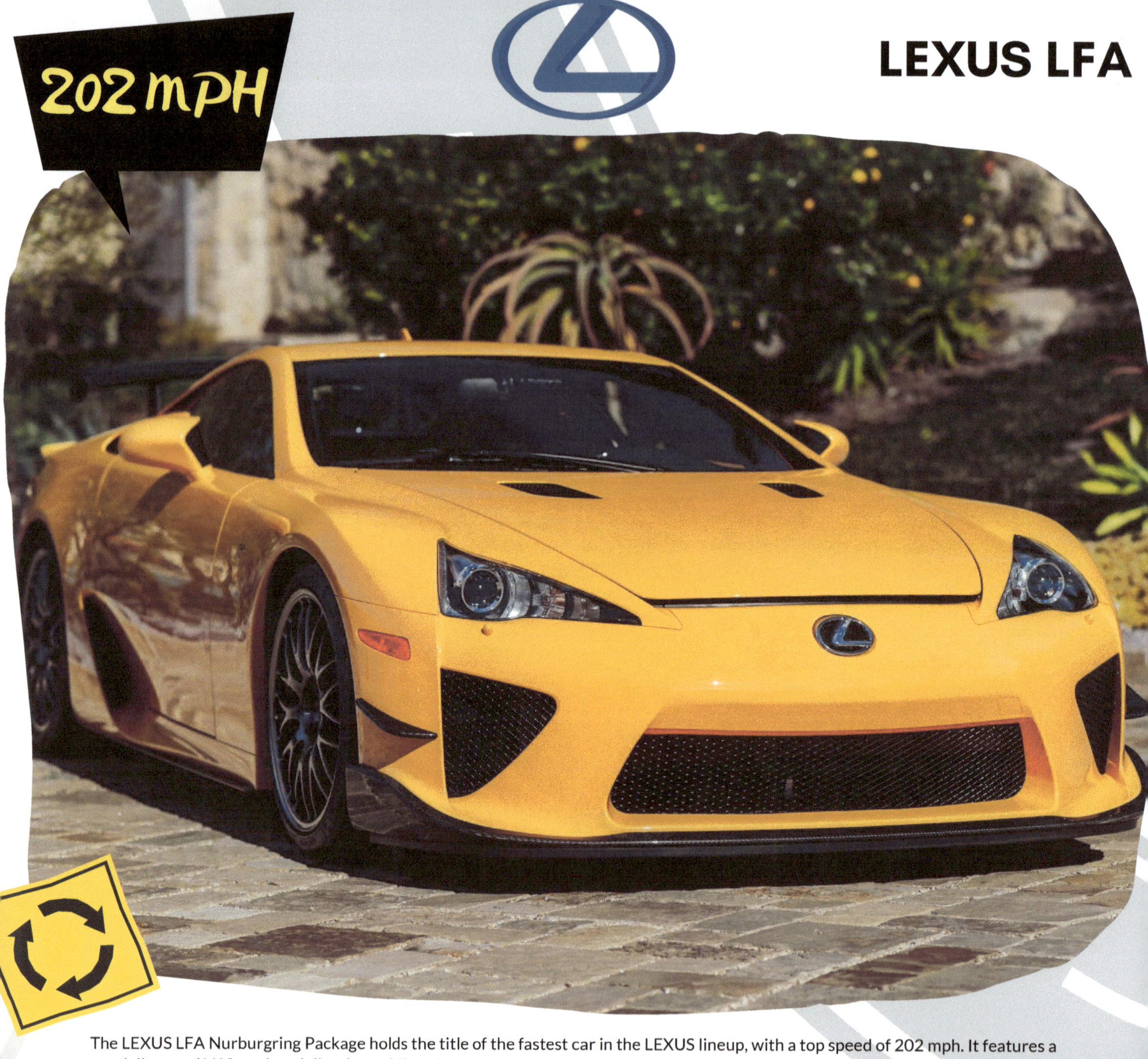

The LEXUS LFA Nurburgring Package holds the title of the fastest car in the LEXUS lineup, with a top speed of 202 mph. It features a specially tuned V10 engine, delivering exhilarating power and performance. This limited edition supercar is known for its exceptional handling and precision, making it a favorite among driving enthusiasts.

DODGE Viper SRT

The DODGE Viper SRT 2015 stands as the fastest car in the DODGE lineup, boasting a top speed of 205 mph. Powered by a formidable V10 engine, it delivers thrilling performance on the road. This iconic sports car is celebrated for its raw power and aggressive styling. With its lightweight construction and aerodynamic design, the Viper SRT 2015 offers an exhilarating driving experience for enthusiasts.

AUDI R8
Decennium

Celebrating a decade of V10 excellence, the AUDI R8 Decennium is the fastest car in the AUDI lineup, with a top speed of 205 mph. Its 5.2-liter V10 engine produces an impressive 620 horsepower. This limited-edition model features exclusive design elements and luxurious interiors, highlighting its special status. The R8 Decennium can accelerate from 0 to 60 mph in just 3.1 seconds, making it a true high-performance machine.

ALFA ROMEO 33
Stradale

The ALFA ROMEO Stradale 33 reaches a top speed of 206 mph, making it the fastest car in the ALFA ROMEO lineup. Equipped with a potent V6 engine, it delivers remarkable power and performance. This high-performance sports car is known for its lightweight construction and advanced aerodynamics. The Stradale 33 can accelerate from 0 to 60 mph in just 2.9 seconds, showcasing its impressive speed and engineering.

The MASERATI Ghibli 334 Ultima holds the title of the fastest car in the MASERATI lineup, with a top speed of 207 mph. It is powered by a 3.8-liter twin-turbo V8 engine that produces an impressive 580 horsepower. This high-performance sedan combines luxury and speed, offering an exceptional driving experience. Additionally, the Ghibli 334 Ultima features advanced aerodynamics and a lightweight design, enhancing both its agility and performance.

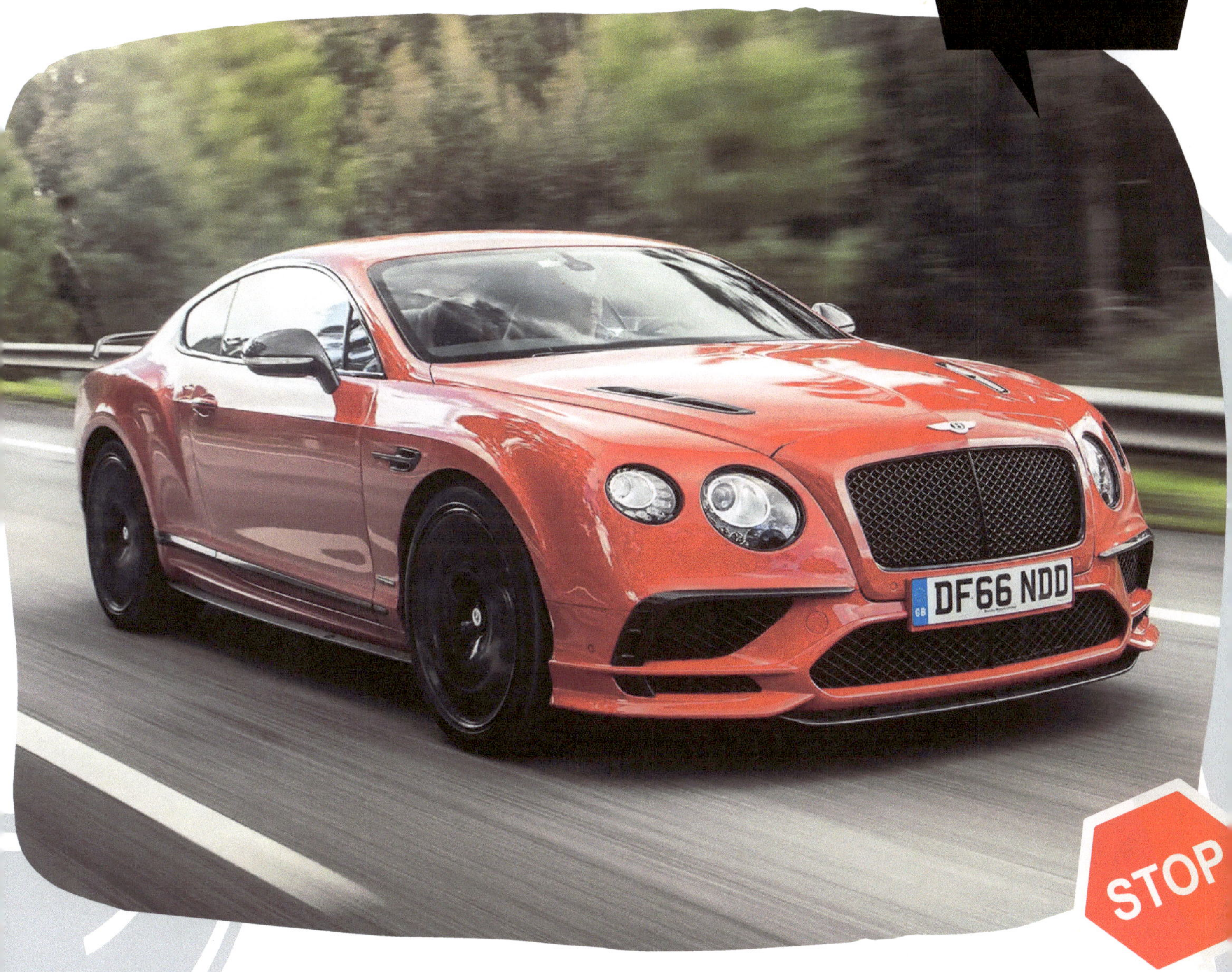

The BENTLEY Continental Supersports is the fastest car in the BENTLEY lineup, with a top speed of 208 mph. It features a 6.0-liter W12 engine that delivers an astounding 700 horsepower. This luxurious yet powerful car can accelerate from 0 to 60 mph in just 3.4 seconds. Despite its performance capabilities, the Continental Supersports maintains the elegance and comfort BENTLEY is renowned for.

The JAGUAR XJ220 reaches a maximum speed of 211 mph, making it the fastest car in the JAGUAR lineup. This iconic supercar is powered by a 3.5-liter twin-turbo V6 engine, producing 542 horsepower. When it was introduced, the XJ220 was the fastest production car in the world. Its sleek design and advanced aerodynamics contributed significantly to its remarkable performance.

PORSCHE 918 Spider

Capable of reaching a top speed of 213 mph, the PORSCHE 918 Spyder is the fastest car in the PORSCHE lineup. This hybrid supercar combines a 4.6-liter V8 engine with electric motors to produce a total of 887 horsepower. It can accelerate from 0 to 60 mph in just 2.5 seconds, showcasing its impressive speed and power. The 918 Spyder also features advanced technology and lightweight materials, making it a marvel of modern engineering.

CHEVROLET CORVETTE ZR1

With a top speed of 213 mph, the CHEVROLET Corvette C7 ZR1 is the fastest car in the CHEVROLET lineup, even outpacing the newer C8 version. It features a supercharged 6.2-liter V8 engine that generates an impressive 755 horsepower. The C7 ZR1 can accelerate from 0 to 60 mph in just 2.85 seconds, demonstrating its remarkable performance capabilities.

FORD GT

Reaching an impressive maximum speed of 216 mph, the FORD GT proudly holds the title of the fastest car in the FORD lineup. With its powerful twin-turbocharged V6 engine, it delivers an exhilarating driving experience. Despite advancements in newer models, the GT remains the epitome of speed and performance for FORD enthusiasts. Its sleek design and advanced aerodynamics contribute to its remarkable speed and agility on the road.

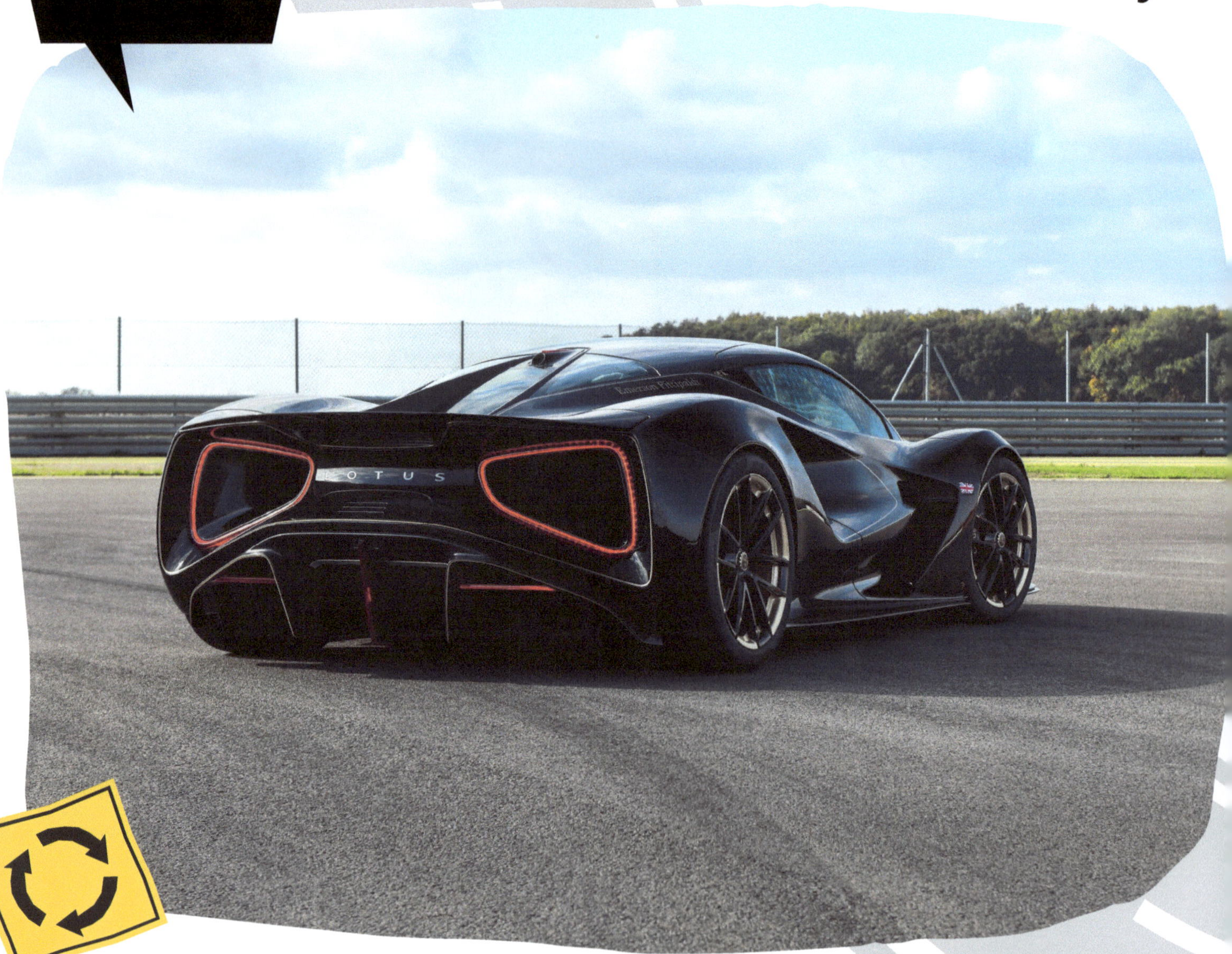

The LOTUS Evija stands as the fastest car in the LOTUS lineup, boasting a top speed of 216 mph. With its electric powertrain, it delivers instantaneous acceleration and impressive performance. This all-electric hypercar is not only quick but also environmentally friendly, showcasing LOTUS's commitment to innovation. Its aerodynamic design and lightweight construction contribute to its remarkable speed and agility on the road.

FERRARI LaFerrari

Clocking in at a top speed of 216 mph, the FERRARI LaFerrari stands as the pinnacle of speed in the FERRARI lineup. Its 6.3-liter V12 engine, combined with an electric motor, delivers a formidable 950 horsepower. This hybrid hypercar boasts a lightweight construction, allowing it to accelerate from 0 to 60 mph in just under 3 seconds.

The MERCEDES AMG One, with a maximum speed of 218 mph, stands as the fastest car of this brand. Its power comes from a hybrid powertrain that includes a 1.6-liter V6 engine combined with electric motors, producing over 1,000 horsepower. Weighing around 3,737 pounds, this car delivers Formula 1 performance in a road-legal package. Additionally, it can accelerate from 0 to 60 mph in just 2.6 seconds, showcasing its incredible speed and power.

NISSAN R390 GTI

The NISSAN R390 GTI, with a top speed of 219 mph, holds the title of the fastest car of its brand. This high-performance vehicle is powered by a 3.5-liter twin-turbo V8 engine. It produces an impressive 550 horsepower, allowing it to achieve remarkable acceleration. Designed for both speed and style, the R390 GTI is a rare and iconic supercar.

The LAMBORGHINI Veneno, with a maximum speed of 220 mph, is the fastest car of its brand. It features a 6.5-liter V12 engine that delivers a staggering 740 horsepower. This supercar can accelerate from 0 to 60 mph in just 2.8 seconds, showcasing its remarkable performance capabilities. Additionally, its lightweight construction and aerodynamic design contribute to its extraordinary speed and agility.

ASTON MARTIN ONE-77

The ASTON MARTIN One-77 boasts a maximum speed of 221 mph, making it the fastest car of its brand. This exceptional vehicle is powered by a 7.3-liter V12 engine, producing 750 horsepower. Its lightweight carbon fiber chassis contributes to its impressive performance and agility. Additionally, the One-77 can accelerate from 0 to 60 mph in just 3.5 seconds, highlighting its remarkable speed.

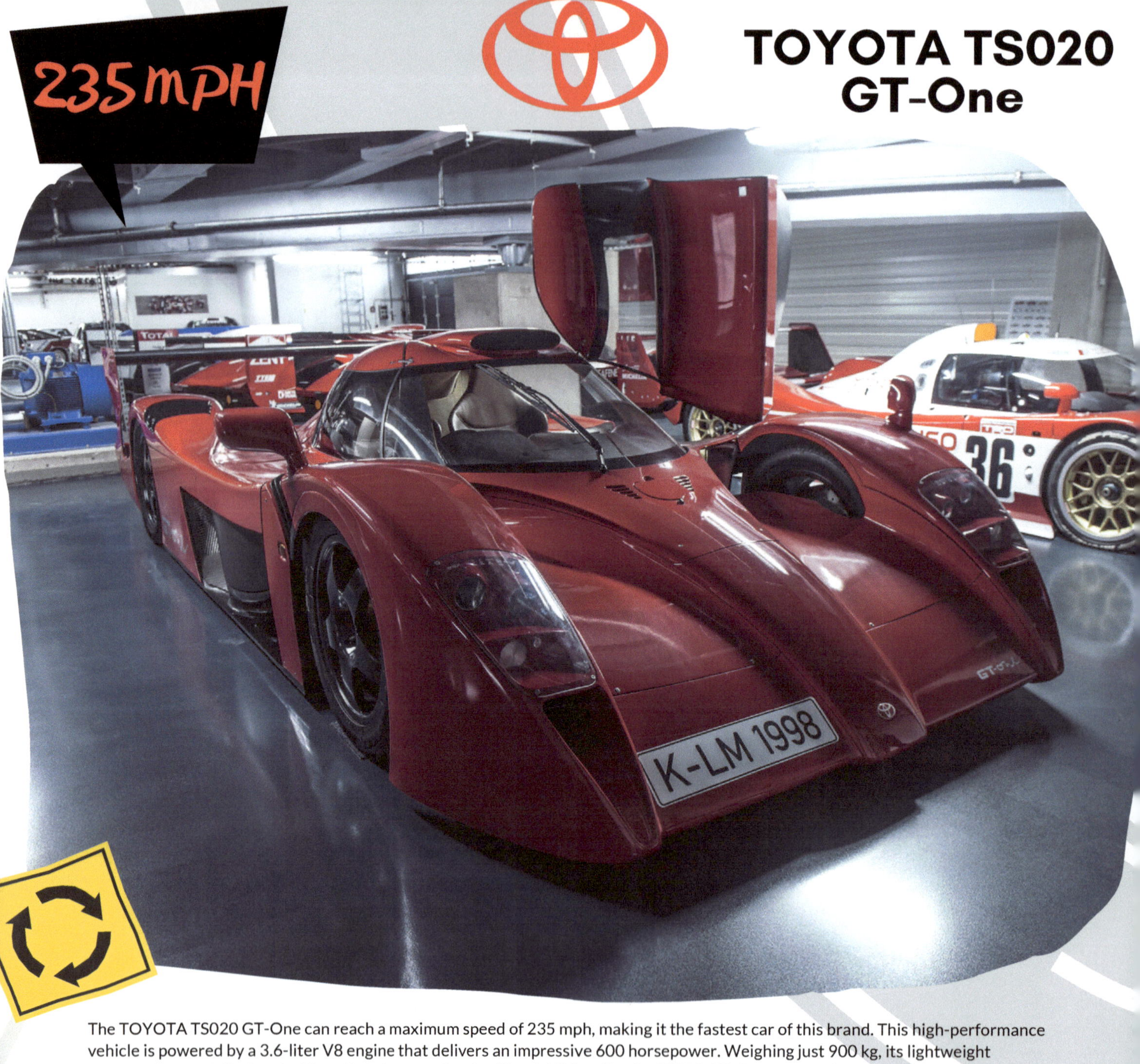

The TOYOTA TS020 GT-One can reach a maximum speed of 235 mph, making it the fastest car of this brand. This high-performance vehicle is powered by a 3.6-liter V8 engine that delivers an impressive 600 horsepower. Weighing just 900 kg, its lightweight construction contributes significantly to its speed and agility. Additionally, the TS020 GT-One can accelerate from 0 to 60 mph in under 3 seconds, showcasing its exceptional acceleration capabilities.

PAGANI Huayra BC Roadster

With a top speed of 239 mph, the PAGANI Huayra BC Roadster stands as the fastest car of this brand. Powered by a mighty 6.0-liter twin-turbocharged V12 engine, it generates an astounding 791 horsepower. Despite its powerful performance, the Huayra BC Roadster maintains a relatively lightweight construction, enhancing its agility on the road. Its acceleration from 0 to 60 mph is an impressive feat, accomplished in just under 3 seconds.

Boasting a remarkable top speed of 249 mph, the MCLAREN Speedtail holds the title of the fastest car of this brand. Its hybrid powertrain, featuring a 4.0-liter twin-turbocharged V8 engine coupled with an electric motor, produces a staggering 1,070 horsepower. The Speedtail's sleek and aerodynamic design contributes to its exceptional performance, allowing it to effortlessly slice through the air. With its acceleration from 0 to 60 mph in just 2.5 seconds, the Speedtail delivers an exhilarating driving experience unlike any other.

ZENVO TSR-GT

Capable of reaching an astonishing top speed of 263 mph, the ZENVO TSR-GT claims the title of the fastest car from this brand. Powered by a formidable 5.8-liter twin-supercharged V8 engine, it delivers exhilarating performance. Despite its speed, the TSR-GT remains a masterpiece of engineering, boasting a sleek and aerodynamic design. With its lightweight construction and advanced technology, this supercar exemplifies the pinnacle of automotive innovation.

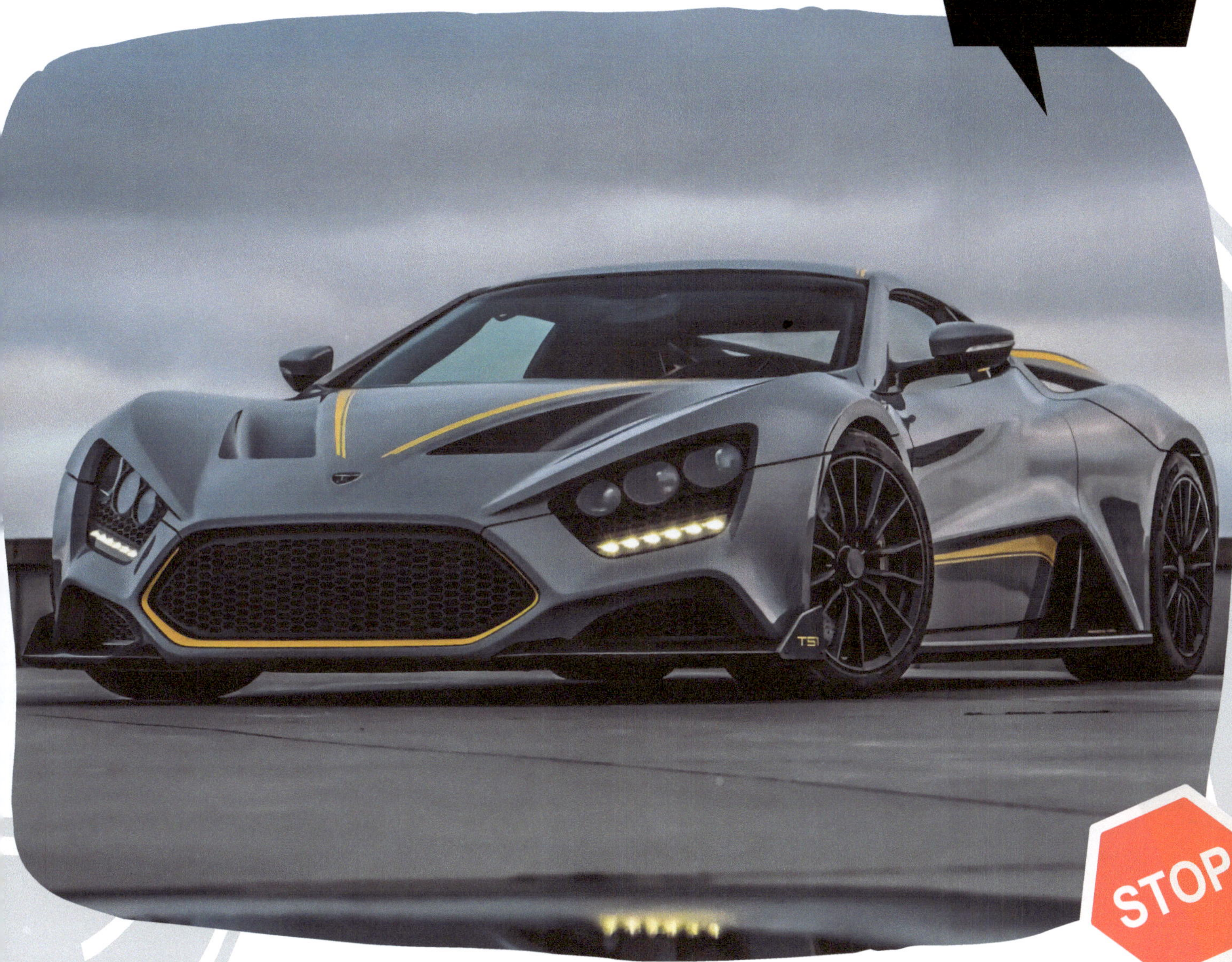

Reaching a mind-bending maximum speed of 295 mph, the SSC Tuatara holds the title as the fastest car from this brand. Propelled by a mighty 5.9-liter twin-turbocharged V8 engine, it produces an awe-inspiring amount of power. Despite its blistering performance, the Tuatara boasts a lightweight carbon fiber construction, contributing to its agility and speed. With cutting-edge aerodynamics and engineering, this supercar pushes the boundaries of automotive excellence.

HENNESSEY VENOM F5

With a staggering maximum speed of 300 mph, the HENNESSEY Venom F5 stands as the fastest car in its brand's lineup. Powered by a monstrous twin-turbocharged V8 engine, that produces over 1,817 horsepower, making it one of the most powerful production cars ever built. Despite its impressive performance, the Venom F5 boasts a relatively lightweight construction, aiding its agility and speed.

The BUGATTI Chiron Super Sport 300+ boasts an astonishing top speed of 304 mph, setting a new standard for hypercars. Its quad-turbocharged W16 engine produces a remarkable 1,577 horsepower, ensuring breathtaking acceleration and performance. Despite its immense power, the Chiron Super Sport 300+ maintains impressive handling and stability, thanks to advanced aerodynamics and suspension technology.

KOENIGSEGG
Jesko Absolut

With a blistering top speed of 329 mph, the KOENIGSEGG Jesko Absolut holds the title of the fastest production car in the world. Powered by a twin-turbocharged V8 engine generating over 1,600 horsepower, it offers unparalleled acceleration and performance. Despite its incredible speed, the Jesko Absolut features advanced aerodynamics to ensure stability and control at high velocities. Its lightweight carbon fiber construction contributes to its agility and responsiveness, making it a true engineering marvel.

Check also:

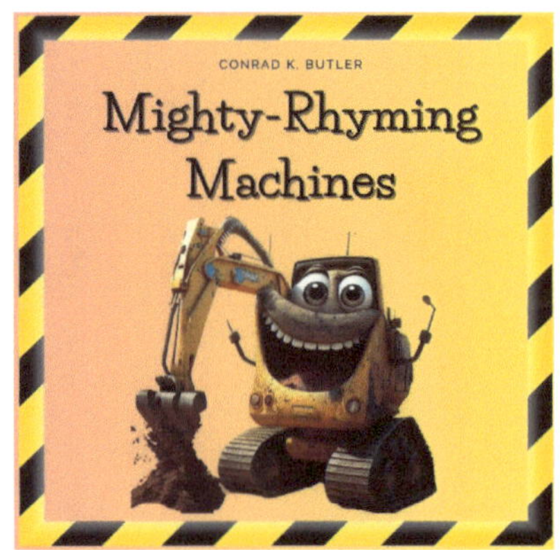

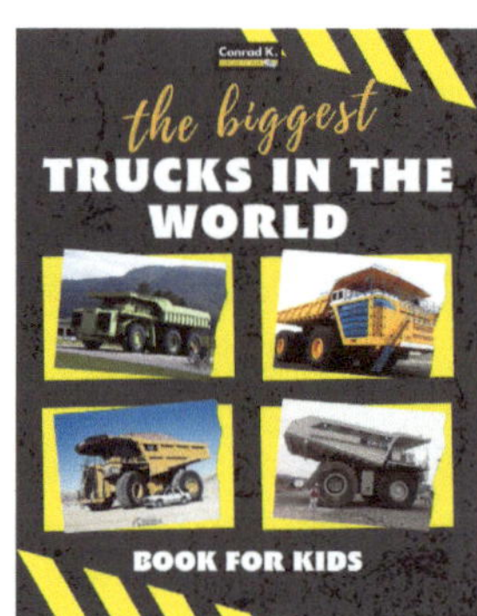

and much more!